I. S. A. M. Special Publications: Number 2

Physiology of the Opera

SCRICI

New Introduction by
D. W. Krummel
University of Illinois

I. S. A. M. Special Publications: Number 2

Physiology of the Opera

SCRICI

New Introduction by
D. W. Krummel
University of Illinois

Institute for Studies in American Music
Department of Music
Brooklyn College
of the City University of New York

An I.S.A.M. Reprint Edition

Library of Congress Catalog Card No. 81-81546
ISBN 0-914678-16-7

Printed in the United States of America

Published by Institute for Studies in American Music
Department of Music
Brooklyn College of the City University of New York
Brooklyn, New York 11210

INTRODUCTION

Italian opera has flourished through applause to the ear and through bouquets to the feet; and also, if the truth be known, through pies to the face. Its conventions have been to the parodist like flames to the moth, like statistics to the social scientist, like honey to the Pooh-Bear; and the greater its success (which has been considerable) the greater its vulnerability to the excesses (and these have also been considerable) which make for good parody.

The European tradition of ridicule, highlighted by Benedetto Marcello's fine *Il teatro alla moda* (*ca.* 1720), is justly celebrated, but America's contribution to the literature has been virtually unknown. Occasional disparagements aside, our country's critics have been preoccupied elsewhere—and, we suspect, too serious and tense to relish properly the rich possibilities at hand. It is thus a pleasant surprize to be reminded of the brief text which is here reproduced. Scrici was no Mark Twain: but then who was? Nor is it fair to call him an urban Artemus Ward, or a perfumed Petroleum Nasby. His levity in fact wears rather well. Its understatement still bears a good chuckle, as its subject matter remains a continuing part of our musical experience.

The single known attribution of the author's excruciating pseudonym is provided in Allibone's *Critical Dictionary* of 1874, where the name of John H. Swaby (elsewhere: Swabey) is exposed. Allibone undermines his own authority by rendering the title as "Philosophy of the Opera"; but he is known to have been a close associate of Hazard, the publisher, and one must presume him to be correct until he is proven wrong, or until the matter can be shown to be of some special consequence which I have not envisioned. The Philadelphia directories do indeed list Swaby between 1850 and 1891. On this basis, and considering the youthful ebullience of his prose, we may guess that he was born in the early 1820s. From his name, we may surmise south-German origins for his family; but noting the way the name is anglicized, we may further speculate that John was no longer a member of any true German community around Philadelphia.

In the early 1850s Swaby is identified as an attorney. But he probably soon discovered what is readily apparent from his text: that his *forte* was high spirits rather than convincing and clean logic. In any event, he soon found a new career, as a wine merchant. The directories further tell us that he moved often but worked mostly on Chestnut or Walnut Streets, in later years enjoying the luxury of a residence separate from his shop. On October 13, 1863, he became a member of the Musical Fund Society—apparently having been forgiven for his youthful literary efforts by a grateful, or forgetful, city. More than this we know not, apart from some bookplates, in volumes dispersed through the Library Company of Philadelphia, identifying books from his estate in 1892.

Scrici's publisher is perhaps even more important to our understanding of his book. Willis Hazard issued mostly children's books and gift editions. Typically small in format and probably in press run as well, they were nicely illustrated and are pleasant to handle, ostensibly timeless in their contents but in fact well calculated, in their graphic conception, to suit current tastes. It is attractive to conjecture that the text was in fact the concoction of several persons, perhaps including Hazard himself, working under conditions similar to those described in Chapter 9, Swaby having provided the congenial context and the dialectic.

Just as the persona of Scrici is a very tenuous matter, so the bibliographical record of his book is less than reassuring. In its day it was advertised neither in *Norton's Literary Gazette* nor in *Dwight's Journal of Music.* It is missing from all the lists of writings on American music, opera, stage, or satire that I know about. There seem to be only six copies known today, four recorded in the National Union Catalog and two in private hands, my own resulting from a warm endorsement by Irving Lowens during a prowl through the Washington, D.C., used-book shops sometime in the 1950s.

Scrici's operatic milieu was youthful, at once self-conscious and boisterous, its institutions as affluent as they were insecure. Italian opera in America was barely a generation old, its origins dating from the famous visit of the Garcìa troupe in 1825. A brief Italian season took place in Philadelphia in 1833-34. In 1841 Bellini's *Norma* was performed in an English version by William Henry Fry and his brothers, and in 1845 Fry's own Italianate *Leonora* was introduced, this being the first grand opera by an American composer. By mid-century New York was clearly the center of American opera, most of the companies headquartering there and touring to other cities like Philadelphia. On September 11, 1851, Jenny Lind made her first American appearance; and Adelina Patti, age 8, made her concert debut in 1852. That year also saw the founding of *Dwight's Journal,* and Fry's return from Paris and the initiation of his celebrated lecture series calling for a native American art music. Such sentiments and Scrici notwithstanding, Italian opera of course ploughed forward with the momentum of a Donizetti *cabaletta.* The text described in Chapter 8 (to my tastes one of Scrici's best) is Verdi's *Ernani,* first heard in Venice in 1844, then introduced to New York in 1846 and to Philadelphia on July 14, 1847. Over the next three seasons, it was heard no fewer than eight times. (Scrici had good reason to be disenchanted.) No Philadelphia performances between 1852 and 1856 are recorded. (Could Scrici have had anything to do with this?) But in 1857 (Scrici being now forgotten?) there were four *Ernani* performances, and over the next two decades nearly a dozen more.

As a parodist Scrici works at various levels. His title is no doubt a reflection on James Rush's celebrated treatise, *The Philosophy of the Human Voice* (Philadelphia 1827; later editions in 1838, 1845, 1855, and 1859), although the two books seem to have absolutely nothing else in common, whether in content, style, or—especially—format. Samuel Rush, perhaps coincidentally, is among the few to follow in Scrici's footsteps, although his essay on singers (dated February 28, 1859, and preserved in his manuscript commonplace book in the American Philosophical Society) is by comparison poorly informed, vindictive, dull, and silly. ("Were I Emperor, I would seize [public singers], have them beaten with many stripes, *jail* them for six months and then banish them to the vilest end of the earth.") Scrici calculates his devastation with more skill and sympathy, so that, after introductory matters are disposed of, each of the main voice-ranges gets her or his own chapter. (For some reason, however, he fails to insult the various maids and rival lovers who inhabit the contralto range. The conductor also makes good his escape.) Scrici's final chapter pays the standard disrespects to opera's attendant fops and dandies; but as a social critic Scrici is most disappointing. (He may never even have heard of the Irish potato famine, let alone of Karl Marx.) What is evident is that he had attended a good many performances and was probably even allowed backstage on a few occasions, his penchant for the female ankle notwithstanding. He is above all the happy and loyal opera fan, anxious mostly to spread such happiness and strengthen such loyalty as could be enhanced by the trappings of psychological distance.

D. W. K.
Urbana, December 1980

SOURCES

Albrecht, Otto E. "Philadelphia." In *The New Grove Dictionary of Music and Musicians* (London: Macmillan, 1980), vol. 14, pp. 622-3.

Allibone, Samuel Austin. *Critical Dictionary of English Literature and British and American Authors.* Philadelphia: J. B. Lippincott, 1858-91.

Armstrong, W. G. *Record of the Opera at Philadelphia.* Philadelphia: Porter & Coates, 1884.

Lahee, Henry C. *Annals of Music in America.* Boston: Marshall Jones, 1922.

__________. *Grand Opera in America.* Boston: L. C. Page, 1902.

Madeira, Louis C. *Annals of Music in Philadelphia and History of the Musical Fund Society.* Philadelphia: J. B. Lippincott, 1896; repr. New York: Da Capo Press, 1973.

Musical Fund Society of Philadelphia. *Acts of Incorporation . . . and By-Laws.* [Philadelphia 1930].

Upton, William Treat. *William Henry Fry, American Journalist and Composer-Critic.* New York: Thomas Y. Crowell, 1954.

The copy reproduced here has been generously provided by the Library Company of Philadelphia. Special thanks are due to Ms. Marie E. Korey and Jennifer B. Lee of the Library Company staff, also for various reference assistance to Frederick James Kent of the Free Library of Philadelphia and to Peter J. Parker of the Historical Society of Pennsylvania.

PHYSIOLOGY

OF

THE OPERA.

BY SCRICI.

PHILADELPHIA.
WILLIS P. HAZARD, 178 CHESNUT ST.
1852.

"I both compose and perform Sir: and though I say it, perhaps few even of the profession possess the *contra-punto* and the *chromatic* better."

CONNOISSEUR. No. 130.

"I see, Sir—you
Have got a travell'd air, which shows you one
To whom the opera is by no means new."

BYRON.

Physiology of the Opera.

Introduction.

S an introduction to the dissertation upon which we are about to enter, such an antiquarian view of the subject might be taken as would tend to establish a parallel between the ancient Greek tragedy and the modern sanguinary Italian opera, the strong resemblance therein being displayed of Signor Salvi trilling on the stage, to the immortal Thespis jargoning from a dung-cart. But we shall indulge in no such wearying pedantry. Our intention being merely to "hold the mirror up to nature," in presenting our immaterial reflector to the public, we invite our readers to a view of the present only—a period of time in which they take most interest, since they adorn it with their own presence.

We feel satisfied that few of the ladies who take a peep into this mirror, will find any cause to break it in a fit of petulancy after having looked upon the attractive reflection of their own lovely features. Few young gentlemen will throw down a glass that gives them a just idea of their striking and distingué appearance behind a large moustache and a gilded *lorgnette.* Old papas, who rule 'change and keep a "stall," cannot be offended with that which teaches them how dignified and creditable is their position, as they sit up proudly and exhibit their family's extravagance and ostentation as an evidence of the stability of their commercial relations. Few mammas will carp at a book which assures them that society does not esteem them less highly because they use an opera box as a sort of matrimonial show window in which they place their beautiful daughters, "got up regardless of expense," as delicate wares in the market of Hymen.

In these our humble efforts to present to our readers an amusing yet faithful picture of the opera, we hope our manner of treating the subject has been to nothing extenuate nor aught set down in malice. This book has not for its end the unlimited censure of foreign opera singers, or native opera goers. We do not therefore, expect to gratify the malignant demands of persons of over-strained morality, who maintain that the opera is a bad school of musical science, or a worse school of morals; and exclaim with the very correct Mr. Coleridge, who was *shocked* in a—*concert room,*

"Nor cold nor stern my soul, yet I detest
These scented rooms; where to a gaudy throng,
Heaves the proud harlot her distended breast,
In intricacies of laborious song.

"These feel not music's genuine power, nor deign
To melt at nature's passion-warbled plaint;
But when the long-breath'd singer's up-trilled strain
Bursts in a squall—they gape for wonderment."

Neither do we coincide in sentiment with those

who, conceiving that every folly and absurdity sanctioned by fashion, is converted into reason and common sense, believe that "the whole duty of man" consists in *spending the day* with Max Maretzeck on the occasion of his musical jubilees, and being roasted by gas in the hours of broad day-light. Consequently the reader will find no one line herein written with the intention of flattering the vanity of those who ride to the opera every night in a splendid coach, followed by spotted dogs.

Having thus declared the impartial manner in which it is our purpose to pursue the physiological discussion of our subject, and the various phenomena involved in its consideration, we proceed at once to unveil the operatic existence to the reader, fatigued no doubt by an introductory salaam already protracted beyond the limits of propriety.

CHAPTER I.

The Opera in the Abstract.

"L' Opéra toujours
Fait bruit et merveilles:
On y voit les sourds
Boucher leurs oreilles."

BERANGER.

TO most of the world (and we say it advisedly,) the opera is a sealed book. We do not mean a bare representation with its accompanying screechings, violinings and bass-drummings. Everybody has seen that—But the race of beings who constitute that remarkable combination; their feelings, positions, social habits;

their relation to one another; what they say and eat;* whether the tenor ever notices as they (the world) do, the fine legs of the contralto in man's dress, and whether the basso drinks pale ale or porter; all these things have been hitherto wrapped in an inscrutable mystery. In regard to mere actors, not singers, this feeling is confined to children; but the operators of an opera are essentially esoteric. They are enclosed by a curtain more impenetrable than the Chinese wall. You may walk all around them; nay, you may even know an inferior artiste, but there is a line beyond which even the fast men, with all their impetuosity, are restrained from invading.

You walk in the street with a young female, on whom you flatter yourself you are making an impression; suddenly she cries out, "Oh, there's Bawlini; do look! dear creature, is'nt he?" You may as well turn round and go home immediately; the rest of your walk won't be worth half the dream you had the night before. This shows an importance to be attached to these remarkable

* We actually knew a man who, when a tenor was spoken of, as having gone through his *role*, thought that that worthy had been eating his breakfast.

persons, which, together with the mystery which encircles them, is exceedingly aggravating to the feelings of a large body of respectable citizens. Among those who are mostly afflicted, we may mention all women, but most especially boarding school misses. Mothers of families are much perturbed; they wonder why the tenor is so intimate with the donna, considering they are not married; and fathers of families wonder "where under the sun that manager gets the money to pay a tenor twelve hundred dollars a month, when state sixes are so shockingly depressed." We were going to enumerate those we thought particularly afflicted by a praiseworthy desire to know something more of these obscurities, but they are too many for us. In every class of society, nay, in the breast of almost every person, there exists a desire to be rightly informed on these subjects. It was to supply this want that we have devoted ourselves more especially to the actors who do, to the exclusion of the auditors who are "*done.*"

Shakspeare observes, that "all the world's a stage;" the converse of this proposition is no less worthy of being regarded as a great moral truth, —that all the stage is a world. Every condition of life may be found typified in one or other of the officials or attachés of an opera house; from the king upon the throne, symbolized by the haughty and magisterial impresario, to the *chiffonier* in the gutter, represented by the unfortunate chorister who is attired as a shabby nobleman on the stage, but who goes home to a supper of leeks. Between these two degrees, of dignity and unimportance, come those many shades of social position corresponding to the happy situations of Secretary of State, Secretary of the Treasury, and divers other dignitaries, set forth in the stage director, the treasurer, the chorus-master, &c.

The tenor, basso, prima donna and baritone may be considered as belonging to what is called "society;"—that well-to-do and ornamental portion of the community, who having no vocation save to frequent balls, soirées, concerts and operas, and fall in love—serve as objects of admiration to those persons less favoured by fortune, who make the clothes and dress the hair of the former class.

Our simile need not be carried further, it being apparent to the most inconsiderate reader, that it is quite as truthful as that hatched by the swan of Avon. We shall now commence our observations upon the most interesting members of a troupe; those best known to the community before whom they nightly appear; and leave unnoticed those disagreeable but influential ones who raise the price of tickets, or stand in a little box near the door and palm off all the back seats upon the uninitiated.

CHAPTER II.

Of the Tenore.

"In short, I may, I am sure, with truth assert, that whether in the *allegro* or in the *piano*, the *adagio*, the *largo* or the *forte*, he never had his equal."—CONNOISSEUR. No. 130.

"Famed for the even tenor of his conduct, and his conduct as a tenor."
KNICKERBOCKER.

THE Tenor is a small man, seldom exceeding the medium height. His voice is, comparatively speaking, a small voice, and consequently not likely to issue from overgrown lungs. His proportions are, or at least ought to be, as symmetrical as possible. His hair, nine times out of ten, is black, and *always* curls. His beard is reasonably bushy; but his moustache is the most artistically cultivated and carefully nurtured collection of hair that ever adorned the superior lip of man. His features are likely to be handsome, sometimes, however, effeminately so. His dress is a little extravagant; not extravagant in the mode and manner of a dandy—for it is not punctiliously fashionable like that of the latter, without any deviation from tailor's plates; neither does it resemble that of the former in the gentlemanly roughness of its appearance; consequently he rejoices not in entire suits of grey or plaid, those *very* sporting coats, those English country-gentleman's shoes, those amply bowed cravats, and those shirts that are so resplendent with the well executed heads of terrier dogs. No! the primo tenore has a passion, first, for satin,—secondly, for jewelry,—and lastly, for hats, boots and gloves. He dotes on satin scarfs, cravats and ties, and his gorgeous satin vests, of all the hues of the rainbow, astound the saunterer on the morning promenade. His love for pins, studs, rings and chains is almost enough to lead us to believe that his blood is mingled with that of the Mohawks. Boots that fit like gloves, and gloves that fit like the skin, render him the envy of dandies. His hat is smooth and glossy to an excess, and its peculiar formation makes it considered "*un peu trop fort*," even by the most daring of hat-fanciers.

The tenor rises late; partly because he is naturally indolent; partly because the primo basso drank him slightly exhilarated the evening previous; and partly out of affectation and the desire to appear a very fine gentleman. Having spent a long time in making a *negligée toilette*, he orders his breakfast. Seated in his comprehensive arm chair, and attired in all the splendor of a well-tinselled satin or velvet *calotte*, a dazzling *robe de chambre*, and slippers of the most brilliant colors, he takes his matutinal repast. And now we begin to discover some of the thousand vexations and annoyances that harass the life of this poor object of popular support. His breakfast is but the skeleton of that useful and nourishing repast. No rich beef-steaks! no tender chops! no fragrant ham nor well-seasoned omelettes, transfer their nutritive properties through his system. Any indulgence in these wholesome articles of food is considered direct destruction to the tender organ of the tenor. A hunting breakfast every day, or a glass of wine at an improper hour, if persisted in for any length of time, it is supposed would ruin the most delightful voice that ever sung an *aria.* A large cup of *café au lait*, with an egg beaten in it, is all the morning meal of which the poor *artiste* (as he styles himself,) is permitted to partake. This feat accomplished, he takes up the newspaper in which he *spells out* the puff which he paid the reporter to insert, and after satisfying himself that he has received his *quid pro quo*, he lounges away the morning until a sufficient space of time has elapsed to render the use of the voice no longer deleterious, as it is immediately after eating. And then come two or three hours of study that is no trifle. The tenor is a man; and it seems to be a great moral law, that whether it come in the form of labor, disease, ennui or indigestion, suffering shall be the badge of all our tribe. Even prima donnas, who defy gods and men with more temerity than all living creatures, are constrained to concede the obligation of this universal moral edict. The tenor then yields homage to human nature and the public, in the labor of climbing stubborn scales, rehearsing new operas, and sometimes, though not often, in receiving the impertinence of arrogant prima donnas, during several hours every day. After these fatiguing efforts, he makes his *grande toilette*, and prepares himself to astound the town no less by his personal attractions than by his song. The chief promenade of the city, where he condescends to mete out to highly favoured audiences the treasures of his organ, is made the day-theatre of his glory. Accompanied by his friend the *primo basso*, he saunters along very quietly, attracting the gaze of the curious, and calling forth the passionate remarks of enthusiastic young ladies, who feel it would be a pleasure to die, if they could only leave such a gentleman behind on earth to sing " *Tu che a Dio*," in the event of their being " snatched away in beauty's bloom."

The basso is the chosen male companion of the tenor's walk; firstly, because he is no rival, and secondly, because the gross physical endowments of the former are such as to bring out the latter's symmetrical proportions in such strong relief.

Sometimes the tenor is seen riding out with the prima donna, with whom he is nearly always a favorite. He is the gentlemen who makes himself useful in assisting her to destroy time; he performs for her those thousand and one little delicate attentions for which all women are so truly grateful; and then he sings with her every night those sentimental duos, that necessarily produce their effect upon the feminine bosom.

Whether walking with his gigantic friend, or riding with his fair one, the tenor behaves himself with the greatest propriety and gentlemanlike bearing, excepting always a certain air which leads us to believe that he thinks "too curious old port" of himself. He is more grave, but apparently more vain when on foot, than when seated in the carriage with the prima donna; at which time his gesticulation becomes very animated, sometimes very extravagant; though we must always accord it the attraction of gracefulness.

The time is thus agreeably walked, ridden and "chaffed" away, until the hour for the substantial dinner comes to fortify mankind against the slings and arrows of hunger and tedium. Then the tenor does dare to partake of a few, of what are technically called "the delicacies of the season." But still a restraint is put upon the appetite, for in a few hours more he must go through labours for which the "fulness of satiety" would little prepare him. A very worthy and elderly clergyman of the Church of England once made known to the writer his opinion concerning after-dinner sermons, in the following words; "I believe, sir, that though sermons preached through the medium of simple roast beef and plum-pudding may have been sermons invented by inspiration; they are sure to be enunciated through the agency of the devil." So melting strains of solos and duos, when sung through the medium of soups, patés and fricasées, lose their liquidity, and film, mantle and stagnate into monotony. How the tenor is occupied until the hour of supper, we shall relate in another chapter; suffice it to say that he is at home—that is to say, on the stage.

But when supper comes he is no longer prevented by fear of "lost voice" or any other dire calamity, from giving way to the cravings of hunger and thirst. He eats with the relish of hunger induced by labor, and drinks with the excitement arising from the consciousness that he is, what in the language of the turf is styled "the favorite." The ladies and gentlemen of the troupe usually assemble at supper, and it is then that the tenor again bestows his *galanteries* on the prima donna, and says many more really complimentary things than are to be found set down in his professional role.

In concluding this sketch of the tenor, the writer would, with all due submission to the opinion of the public, venture to discover his sentiments upon a question which often agitates society; viz., whether the tenor is always sick when he announces himself to be seriously indisposed. The writer hopes he will not render himself liable to the charge of duplicity or an attempt at evasion, when he declares it to be his impression, that on the occasion of such announcements, the tenor is *sometimes* seriously indisposed but not *always*. The tenor, as we have before observed, is but a man, and must needs be subject to diseases like other men ; but when we consider the delicacy of his conformation, we must multiply the chances of his liability to indisposition. His organization is such, that the most trifling irregularity in his general health operates immediately upon the voice. Now, for the tenor, in the slightest degree out of tone, to appear before a merciless audience, consisting of blasé opera goers, tyrannical critics, hired depreciators, and unrelenting musical amateurs, would indicate the most utter folly and imbecility. The tenor is well aware that a reputation for singing divinely a few nights in the year, is more lucrative than a reputation for ability to sing tolerably well, taking an average of all the nights in that space of time. It is consequently more advantageous for him to sing occasionally, when he feels his voice to be in full force and vigour, and his spirits in a sufficiently animated condition to warrant his appearing with every certainty of success. When, therefore, he does not favour the public with the melody of his notes, it is, generally speaking because, without really suffering from a serious attack of disease, he considers that his appearance would insure a future diminution in the offers of the *impresario.* Hence the *affiches* usually proclaim nothing but truth itself, when they declare that the tenor is *seriously indisposed;* but then we must be careful to interpret the word indisposition by that one of its significations which is equivalent to *disinclination.*

That some compulsory measures might be taken to make these gentlemen "who can sing but won't sing" more complying, and willing to yield to the wishes and request of managers and audiences, the writer has never entertained a doubt. The ways and means of effecting such an object, he will not take upon himself to devise or advise, but will merely state a fact which probably may induce some one to enter upon a thorough examination of the subject, and suggest the remedy. Upon one occasion, when the Havannah troupe was performing in Philadelphia, and a favorite tenor had been amusing himself by trifling with the public, until the patience of that forbearing portion of mankind was entirely exhausted; the treasury was beginning to fall extremely low, and the wearied out director was well nigh driven to desperation. In this critical juncture of affairs, the gentleman who was the legal adviser of the troupe was applied to, to say whether there was not some compulsory process known to the law, by which the refractory tenor could be brought to a recognition of the right of the rest of the company to the use of his voice to attract large audiences, and thereby replenish the empty coffers of the treasury. Upon answer that there existed no such process, the distracted director muttered a few maledictions upon our country, with a sneer at our *free institutions*, and informed the astonished counsellor, that in Havannah, when the tenor was supposed to be feigning sickness, the proper authorities were resorted to for the right of an examination of the offending party by a physician, and a certificate of the state of his health. Upon the physician certifying that the signor was able to go through his role, a few *gendarmes* were dispatched to seize the delinquent and take such means as would sooner coerce him into a compliance with the stipulations of his professional contract.

Every reasonable excuse, however, should be made for the necessity the tenor is under to be careful of the delicate organ whereby he gains his subsistence. When we reflect how many of these poor fellows lose their voices and are consequently driven to throw themselves on the cold charity of the public—or out of the window, we must be struck with the inhumanity which would be exercised if this professional singer were excluded from enjoying occasionally by permission, what every clergyman in the land can always claim as a right—the disease which the Hibernian servant expressively denominated "the brown gaiters in the throat."

CHAPTER III.

Of the Primo Basso.

"And for the bass, the beast can only bellow;
* * * *
An ignorant, noteless, timeless, tuneless fellow."

BYRON.

THE Primo Basso is to the primo tenore what the draught horse is to the racer; drawing along the heavy business of an opera, whilst the other goes capering and curvetting through whole pages of chromatics, and runs bounding with unerring precision over the most fearful musical intervals. The basso, consequently, to uphold the vast superstructure of song, must be a man furnished with a strong supporting and sustaining voice. He usually plays the part of tyrants, either of the domestic circle or of the throne; and the tyrants of fiction always have been represented as over-grown individuals, from the time of the Titans down to the giants who met with their well-merited fate from the invincible arm of that doughty nursery hero—*Jack the Giant Killer*. It is a most fortunate circumstance then for the basso, that while his powerful voice must necessarily proceed from gigantic lungs, and these organs again are chiefly found planted in largely developed frames, his huge proportions only the better qualify him for his department of operatic personæ. His form is heavy, and would be muscular, if ease and indolence, unrestrained appetite, and no more exertion than is requisite to blow the bass-bellows during half a dozen evenings in the week, did not permit an undue accumulation of adipose substance. His hair is generally black, but not of that rich, glossy, *curling* kind, which decks the fair brow of the delicate little tenor. His features are gross and sensual, exhibiting about the amount of intelligence which may be looked for in one of those bedecked and garlanded animals, whose appearance among us announces the future sale of show beef. His dress is an exhibition of slovenly grandeur. Each article of clothing is in itself very handsome, perhaps very gaudy; but the manner in which it is dragged on the figure, makes the *tout ensemble* coarse and common, slovenly and disagreeable. His animal propensities hold the intellectual faculties in bondage, and every approach to sentiment is excluded by the clogged up avenues to thought. His manner of living is *sensualité en action.* His life is an existence, tossed and troubled by the vicissitudes of sleeping and feeding, with occasional interruptions of mechanical vocalization. He possesses an organ, which it is supposed cannot be impaired by indulgence in the pleasures of the table, and he always acts as if he wished to put this supposition to the test. When he orders his breakfast, therefore, he does not look down the *carte* in order to see what viands he must avoid, but only to ascertain how many dishes are likely to be objects agreeable to his palate. *Substantials* form all his meals. No mild *café au lait,* composes the meal which is to announce that he has commenced his daily labours of mastication. After a morning's deglutition worthy of the anaconda, he suffers digestion to prepare him for a walk, while he indulges in piles of cigars. As this smoking effort is a long one, he is about ready to join his elegant friend, the tenor, when the latter calls on him to go out and astound the town. What a majestic stride the heavy, beefy fellow puts on as he saunters down the street! How his body seems to say—for his face is void of expression; how his body seems to say; "gentlemen, you're all very well,—but it won't do; I out-weigh a dozen of you, and the ladies have to surrender to such a superior weight of metal."

The basso seldom loves the prima donna. He regards her as a very troublesome lady, who *devils* him at rehearsals, because he won't sing in time; on the stage, because she wants to show her importance; and in the *salon*, because she requires so much attention.

The only wonder is, how he and the delicate, sensitive tenor, persons presenting such a decided contrast to each other, should live together on terms of such apparent friendship. The reason, however, is, that the association is not one arising from choice, but from necessity. Between the tenor and the baritone, there is a something too much of similarity in voice and *physique* to render them just the most inseparable friends in the world; but in the vast musical gulf between the tenor and the basso, all professional rivalry is buried.

CHAPTER IV.

Of the Prima Donna.

"Your female singer being exceedingly capricious and wayward, and very liable to accident."—SKETCH BOOK.

EVERY body knows what a prima donna is. She is the *first lady*, and this is a fact apparently better known to the individual herself, than to any body else—at least her actions would warrant this inference. She deems herself more indispensable to an opera than an executioner to an execution, or the thimbles to a thimble-rig man. She takes no pains to conceal what a high price she sets on the value of her presence. She sings just when she pleases, and just as she pleases. Caprice itself is not more capricious than this fair creature. As capricious as a prima donna has almost become a proverb, and we predict that in a few years it will become fully established as such. She is a female tyrant. Impresario, treasurer, chef (d' orchestre,) chorus master and chorus tremble before her, when in one of her passions she brings down her pretty little foot in a most commanding stamp. She gives the first mentioned person more trouble than all the singers, orchestra and officials together, with her coughs, colds and affected indispositions. Next to the impresario, the chef (d' orchestre) suffers most from her imperious spirit. He never conducts so as to accompany her properly, and though she sings a half a note higher than she did at rehearsal, she expects every poor musician to transpose his music at sight, or receive the indications of her displeasure in a way that leads the audience to believe that the fault lies entirely with the orchestra. She worries the basso,—poor, heavy, drowsy fellow,—because he's such a slow coach—and such an oaf. She is disposed to be more friendly to the tenor, who is the only person who receives any tokens of her good-will; but in truth, she would cease to be a woman, if she were unkind to this gentlemanly, polite little fellow. Neither does she hold the public in the least regard, but conceives that she has a right to be seriously indisposed as often as she thinks that people are really desirous to hear her; and "is subject when the house is thin, to cold," as Byron says. She keeps all the town who have determined to go and hear her, in the most provoking suspense. Balls and evening parties are sadly interrupted by her erratic course, for she is sure to sing on the evenings assigned to those delightfully laborious modes of destroying time. All the pleasure promising engagements made by the Browns and the Smiths to form a party, and go in concert to the opera, are postponed from time to time, to the great vexation of young Harry Brown, who craftily set the affair on foot, in order to have an evening's "chaff" with Miss Julia Smith.

Sometimes the prima donna's "serious indisposition" is not discovered by the fair singer herself, until the ladies of the audience have removed the cloaks, furs and hoods which guard their loveliness from the cold of a winter night; until the young gentlemen have jammed their opera hats into an inconceivably small space, and adroitly passed the hand up to the collar and cravat to discover how things are in that quarter; and until the old *habitués* have settled themselves down into the softest chair of the pit, with the full intention of being extremely displeased, and making very unfavourable comparisons between the performance about to take place, and one at which they were present some twenty years before. However, she is a splendid creature—a small miracle in the way of humanity—and can therefore be excused from pursuing that monotonous and regular course of life which "patient merit" is obliged to take.

She is either a beautiful woman in reality, or one who can get up such an admirable imitation that it is difficult to distinguish it from from the genuine. She is well skilled in music, at least in its execution; but she is always much more deeply versed in the virtues of cosmetics, and in the art of making herself beautiful.

There are two varieties in the figure of the prima donna; either, firstly, such as to qualify her for opera buffa and certain tragic roles, in which case she is of medium stature, delicate proportions, and possesses the most graceful and vivacious action. Prima donnas of this stamp make the dearest, sweetest, most innocent-looking Aminas; the most sprightly, coquettish Rosinas, and the most faithful, confiding and sincere Lucias. Or, secondly, she is of a large mould, more masculine dimensions, with a countenance that can gather up in a moment a show of the requisite amount of fury to poignard the husband and strangle the *babbies*. She plays all the high tragedy roles, doing the Semiramide, Norma and Lucrezia, with a very sanguinary power and effect. Those of the first kind are most admired by the gay young fellows about town who have no taste for music, and who do not resort to the opera to hear it, but make the parquette a lounging place where they can be in the mode, see beautiful women, and show *themselves*.

The prima donna, in her attempts to render herself personally attractive, has an auxiliary in her maid, who is a compound of companion and servant, and a *coiffeuse* gifted with the most delicate taste and artistic execution. How often have we looked round the house and been forced to confess that the prima donna was literally the *first lady* in the building, in respect to costume and *coiffure*. This maid too, is almost as much of a curiosity among maids as her mistress among fine ladies. She may be regarded as a prima donna without a voice, without fine clothes, bouquets, and a tenor companion ; and it is her *destiny* to marry one of the violinists, when her mistress marries the tenor. It is upon this official that the duty of attending to the prima donna's lap-dogs Beatrice and Amore, particularly devolves—two animals that are almost as dear to their possessor as her professional reputation. In addition to these darling little quadrupeds, upon which so many caresses are bestowed, both by the faultless hand of the mistress, and the same well-diamonded member of the tenor, a parrot usually divides the affections of one, who woman-like, must love something, but who has been so far initiated into the ways of the world as to doubt the sincerity of all mankind, except probably that of the aforesaid tenor. We remember once being present when a well-known prima donna was about to leave a northern city, where a rival cantatrice had lately appeared, and was inducing comparisons unsatisfactory to the former. She had been informed that an overland trip to New Orleans would be greatly incumbered by the presence of her lap-dogs and parrot, and was prevailed on to bestow them on some tender-hearted persons, whose extreme affection for domesticated animals would be a guaranty for their gentle treatment. A married gentleman—we are afraid without having consulted his wife—kindly offered to relieve the lady from all trouble in finding the suitable persons, by taking them himself. Assuming the attitude of Norma handing over babes, she delivered up the poodles. With what sadness were the little creatures confided to his care. What admonitions and instructions to carefully keep them; what prayers for their faithful protection; a womanly tear bedewed the cheek of the fascinating lady, and a smile followed, as if to ask forgiveness for what she feared those present might consider an unbecoming weakness. Five years afterwards, we saw in a concert room this same sensitive creature, who was so moved and affected at the *derniers adieux* paid to her hateful little poodles, scowl darkly, bite her lips, and turn her back on the person who had engaged her, whom, by the by, we, in common with the audience, regarded as a much aggrieved individual.

Between the attention and affection bestowed on her pets, some hours devoted to study and rehearsal, occasional rides and walks, and time

spent in the pleasing avocation of arranging her wardrobe, and in innocently admiring her fair self in the mirror, the days of this spoiled child of the music-loving are whiled away. She is acquainted with some of the dandies of the place where she for the time resides, but as such gentlemen in this country seldom have the temerity to appear with her in public, their usefulness as escort promenaders is greatly abridged. The fast men sometimes smuggle themselves into her visiting circle, in order to be able to boast of their intimacy with the prima donna; but as this class of society is seldom very *fluent* in the use of Italian, and

as there is small affinity between the sentimentality of the opera and "mile heats to harness," this acquaintance is not of very long duration.

The necessity of personal beauty in a prima donna is such, that she must "assume that virtue if she have it not." Not many winters since, a beautiful cantatrice was induced to undertake the role of Romeo in "I Montecchi ed I Capuletti." The lady was excellently proportioned, except that there existed a great want of symmetry in the inferior members; and as Romeo's skirts must necessarily be short, and the lady could not at will assume a pair of well turned knees and calves, she clothed the offending limbs in what, at this day would be called "Bloomer pantaloons." The attempt to ingraft turkish trowsers on the Veronese costume, proved too absurd to warrant the continuance of such a representation, and was abandoned after the night of its introduction.

The effect of a prima donna on society is very various. If she be of the high tragic or strangulation school, it is to induce young ladies of some voice, *and a good deal of person*, to clothe themselves in white *tulle* on the occasion of evening parties and amateur concerts—draw their hair very smoothly over the temples—drive a white camellia into the left side of the head, and sing long recitatives from Norma or Lucrezia;—in the case of evening parties to the infinite chagrin cf young gentlemen possessed of great waltzing powers and passions; and in the case of amateur concerts, to the fatigue of yawning audiences. If the prima donna is of the coquettish school of song, every damsel of sylph-like proportions, vivacious expression, and a turn for man-killing, chirps and warbles away in the sprightly passages of the *Barbiere*.

As for the male part of the community, it is perfectly easy to divine how they will be affected by the appearance of the different "*prime donne*" who from year to year present themselves for musical honors. They will always be pleased, but chiefly by those who are rather attractive in features than in voice. The very young and inexperienced men just entering into society, denominated "cubs" by the beaux of some years standing, affect most the prima donna of the sanguinary school, because she seems more in accordance with the ideas they have derived from the study of Medéa, a work to which they have not long since bid adieu. They regard the killing of babes as the most tragic of tragedy, and the actress who can do the thing best, as the most accomplished of actresses. But the knowing fellows of mature years prefer the pretty creatures who look so fond and affectionate, in their short peasant dresses, displaying the delicate little foot and well turned ancle. How they gather night after night into the parquette, to compare opinions on the merits of Orsini's soft notes, and the long, beautifully-filled stockings of the page dress. We once heard an enthusiastic Cuban remark, when Patti was singing Orsini to Parodi's Lucrezia; "Parodi is the finest singer I ever heard, —she is the best actress I ever saw; some few people can appreciate her singing, many more her acting;—but Patti's legs! Ah! Sir, that is something that everybody can understand." How delighted the young fellows pretend to be with the wild, bacchanal song, when in reality they only encore the songstress, in order to have another opportunity of admiring her pretty knees. Alas, how foolish they are to throw away admiration on one who takes no more thought of them than if they never existed; but each one of them supposes that she must necessarily, be slightly enamoured of him-

self. The consequence is, that next morning divers bouquets, with small notes or cards containing a few amatory words, appended to them, are handed in to the servant, who is very much out of humour at what has become troublesome from its over repetition.

The old *habitués*, of course, will not be affected in any way except by peevishness and petulance, which will drive them into their usual course of detraction. "Ah!" says old Twaddle; "Pasta—you should have seen Pasta! No melodramatic twaddle about her! Genuine, artistic delineation of passion and profound emotion. And then what a voice! none of your ambiguous voices there; no difficulty in pronouncing, whether soprano or contralto. And then her beauty—none of your namby-pamby, sickly, insignificant prettiness." And thus Twaddle grumbles on, making shocking comparisons between the past and present. Poor old Twaddle! he has, according to his own showing, outlived all that is good in the province of music.

The prima donna in this country will, generally speaking, produce on any foreigner who happens to be among us, an effect very much akin to that exercised upon Twaddle. She will set him sighing after the vocalization of the other side of the Atlantic. He will seem to forget that Parodi or "the Hays" ought to sing as well in this country as in Europ. But still he can't be brought to that belief; and what is worse, upon your venturing to suggest any possibility of such a state of the case, you are made to perceive that he considers that your nationality puts you off the bench of musical critics.

Query. Why is it that *every* Frenchman is supposed to be an infallible judge of sweet sounds? For our own part, we no more believe that every Gallic gentleman is fit for a critic, than that every one can raise a handsome moustache.

Another effect of a beautiful prima donna, is to make young husbands, who have been married *just* two years, look so steadfastly on the stage, that their young wives sit with their eyes fastened on a cousin George or Harry, in the parquette.

CHAPTER V.

Of the Barytone.

"Our Barytone I almost had forgot;
* * * *
In lover's parts, his passion more to breathe,
Having no heart to show, he shows his teeth."—BYRON.

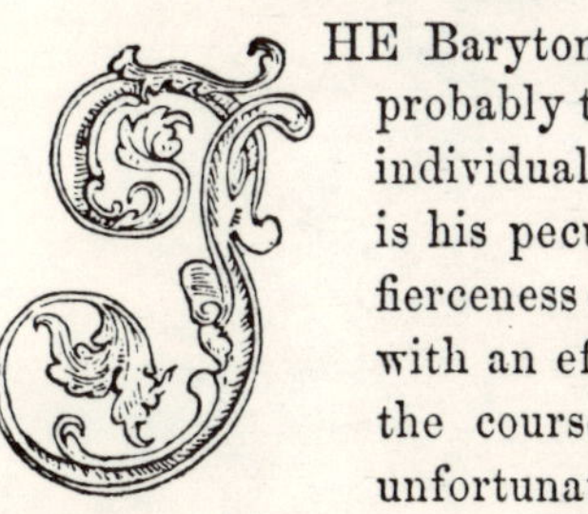

HE Barytone of the opera is probably the most inoffensive individual in the world. This is his peculiarity. Even his fierceness on the stage is done with an effort; and when in the course of a piece he is unfortunately called on to massacre somebody, we always fancy that he does it with the most unfeigned reluctance, and for aught we know, with silent tears. He is generally of a bashful, retiring disposition, and pretty nearly always awkward. This perhaps arises from the anomalous position he occupies in operatical society. He cannot be on good terms with the basso,—they have too much similarity in their voices for that; he is on no more friendly relations with the tenor for the same reason. Besides never daring to aspire to the familiarity with the prima donna which that worthy enjoys, he suffers under the affliction of conscious diffidence in their presence.

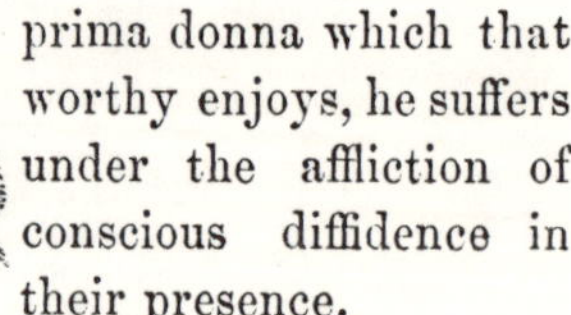

The barytone must as surely be the king as the basso must be the tyrant; indeed we have often thought of the startling effect which would be produced by an opera in which this law of nature was reversed. To hear the lover growling his tender feelings in a gutteral E flat, and moaning his hard lot in a series of double D.'s; to listen to the remorseless tyrant ordering his myrmidons to "away with him to the deepest dungeon 'neath the castle moat," in the most soothing and mellifluous of tenor head notes, would produce such a revulsion in operatic taste, as surely to create a deep sensation, if nothing more.

CHAPTER VI.

Of the Suggeritore or Prompter.

"There never was a man so notoriously abused"
TWELFTH NIGHT.

"But whispering words can poison truth."
COLERIDGE.

WE should be much grieved were we to let a chance of immortality at our hands go by, for our great friend the prompter—the suggeritore of the Italians. The prompter is to the opera, what the fifth wheel is to a wagon; everything rubs, grates and abrades it, yet the whole concern turns on it. He is the most abused (not hated—that is reserved for the Impresario,) man in the company. But he does not care for it. That is what he is hired for. He is paid to be of a good temper, and he does it. He returns docility for dollars; and suavity for salary. He is the true philosopher; just enough in the company to be part of it, and sufficiently detached to avoid all the squabbles and bickerings. He, however, is the victim of all the caprices of the company, from the prima donna, who in a miff kicks about *his partition* in a very piano cavatina, to each of the bandy-legged choristers. True, he has his little revenge. This he accomplishes by using his voice too much and too loudly in the *sotto voce* parts, so that all the duos become trios and the quintettes, choruses. This is little enough to sweeten the embitterments of a *suggeritore's* life, but such it is, and he is contented. The *suggeritore* must be a thin man. It does not require a Paxton to know that a hole in the stage two feet square, will not hold Barnum's obesities. He must also be short and supple-necked, to allow the green fungus which excresces from the stage to cover him; and he must be the fortunate owner of a right arm as untiring as a locomotive crank or the sails of a windmill. It is a prevalent but mistaken idea, that the prompter is an impolite man; we happen to know that it is a matter of the deepest concern with him to be obliged to sit with his back to the audience. But he is like the angels and St. Cecilia, "*Il n'avait pas de guoi*" to do otherwise. Operas must be, singers must have, a led horse—(N. B. How can delicate females and tenors be expected to recollect "*les paroles;*")—and there he is, with a little hole in the back of his calash for the leader of the orchestra to stir him up when the excitement becomes very strong, and the time is irrecoverably lost. As to the social habits of the suggeritore, the naturalist is at a loss, for he immediately disappears after rehearsal, and remains in close retirement till the performance, after which he is again lost till the next day.

CHAPTER VII.

Before the Curtain.

> " A neat, snug study on a winter's night;
> A book, friend, single lady, or a glass
> Of claret, sandwich, and an appetite,
> Are things which make an English evening pass,
> Though *certes* by no means so grand a sight,
> As is a theatre, lit up with gas.—BYRON.

THE night is a cold one; the snow is falling in large, heavy flakes, and those who are fond of the frigid, but exhilarating amusement of sleighing, are in hopes that by the morrow they will be able to pass like lightning from one part of the city to the other, in a sleigh decked with warm, gaily trimmed furs; filled with a merry company, and drawn by two high-headed, dashing trotters. The gas lights are just discernible from corner to corner. The number of people in the streets is steadily decreasing, and the sound of their footfall is muffled in the snow. About the theatres and the opera house, however, crowds of the idle and curious, gaping at those who are entering these buildings, make it necessary for the police to pace to and fro, ordering back the more presumptuous loiterers, who press forward and obstruct the approach to the doors.

Query? Why does the crowd always stare at those who are going into a theatre or opera? The latter are attired somewhat strangely to be sure, but still they don't look *exactly* like Choctaws.

The cab and chaise-men muffled up in their cold-defying great-coats and woolen comforters, are opening the doors of their several vehicles, out of which ladies enveloped in cloaks and hoods are dismounting under cover of umbrellas, held probably by the "best of brothers," but more probably by gentlemen in no way related to them. In the opera house all is bustle and commotion. The officials are selling tickets, receiving tickets, and directing to their places bevies of ladies and gentlemen bewildered in a maze of passages. The audience is impatiently preparing itself for a delightful evening's entertainment. The dandies, who are so unfortunate as not to have accompanied ladies have already brought themselves up to the attack, and have levelled their opera-glasses on all the points where they know well-established objects of admiration are likely to be found. Now and then they bow their recognition in a reserved inclination, or in a careless smiling way that bespeaks the freedom of familiar intimacy.

The fast-men are standing at the doors in knots of three and four, talking over the last trot of Suffolk, or the probable chance of victory in the next day's dog-fight, and making a few, no doubt *very fast*, but not very proper allusions to the shoulders of some rather sparingly habited *belles*. The Cubans in the parquette, who, by the by, during their sojourn in this country will best preserve their liberty by remaining north of Mason and Dixon's line, are clearing their voices in very doubtful Spanish, for those animated bravos, which we must admit they always administer in the very best taste, both as to time and quantity. Here and there, some lone young man, desolate in a crowd, who has seldom before been exposed to the full blaze of the all-discovering gas light, not exactly knowing what to do with himself, is endeavouring, with a fictitious indifference, to fill up the vacancies of attention by smoothing down the stubborn folds of badly selected white *kids*. Five collegians just escaped from the studious universities for a high week in town, have established themselves all together, and commenced a running commentary, carried on chiefly in the Virginia dialect, on men, women, and things, much to the annoyance of a very foreign gentleman behind them—so foreign that he is almost black—who looks stilettos at his cheerful but over-loquacious neighbours. One youth in an excessively white, though unpleasantly stiff cravat, is assisting an equally stiff old chaperon into her place, at the expense of great physical efforts, till his cheeks are thereby suffused with a tint strongly resembling the color of a juvenile beet, while the distended veins of his forehead would make a fine anatomical study for the laborious medical student, if that fabulous biped were still extant. The chaperon being disposed of, four young ladies under her *surveillance*, two in opera cloaks and hoods, and two in antediluvian mantles and pre-adamitic head-gear, assuring the existence of rural cousinship, by four minor efforts of the same gentleman, are at length safely landed in their places. But now commences a new round of confusion. Each of the four young ladies discovers that she has placed herself on some article of clothing belonging to her companion. Whereupon she half rises, and having drawn forth the disturbing habiliment, resumes her former position: and as this movement is performed by each one of them without regard to the order in which they have placed themselves, and is repeated half a dozen times in as many minutes, the unconscious fair ones become the subjects of the allusions of the fast-men, who immediately institute comparisons between them and various animate and inanimate objects. One of these gentlemen observing that their motions remind him of a flock of aquatic fowl, known by the name of divers, a facetious friend replies that probably he means diving bells; which being considered an extremely happy pun, it meets with a hearty laugh of approbation. But an ambitious fast wit, fearing that his reputation is likely to be lost forever, if he remain silent, says that the whole groupe of uneasy females recalls the line of Coleman,

"For what is so gay as a bag full of fleas."

This being regarded as the acme of brilliancy, there is no telling what might be the consequences if their attention were not drawn into another channel by the entrance of a distinguished belle, who is immediately pronounced to be a "stunner" and the question is raised as to who the man is who acts as "bottle holder," reference thereby being had to the gentleman who is so polite as to hand the lady to her place, and aid her in disposing of her divers little appliances of operatic necessity. The *belle* scarcely takes her seat before she commences to hum snatches of Italian airs, in a very careless indifferent way, just to show how much she is at home in such a place, and probably to attract a little more attention.

Query? Why do the handsomest women at an opera *always* talk and laugh the loudest?

That portion of the audience comprised in the gentler sex is here in all the attraction of natural loveliness and adventitious ornament, putting to flight a notion once prevalent, that beauty when unadorned is then adorned the most.

The noise of conversation which now lulls, now swells out in gentle crescendos, is chiefly the production of this taciturn part of the audience. All at once the gas is let on in a gush of light, the buzz of voices, which up to this time has been carried on in a subdued tone, bursts out into full force, with a suddenness that seems to render it probable that the conversation has been issuing all the while from the gas jets. The augmented light brings down another volley from the foci of a thousand *lorgnettes.* At this moment the musicians begin to enter the orchestra which has been void of occupants all the evening, with the exception of one meaningless old fellow, who has been attempting to restore order among the stands, seats, and books, but whose laudable efforts have ended in what every single gentleman at lodgings knows all endeavours to "set things to rights," are sure to effect—a state of affairs in which confusion is considerably worse confounded. But after all a music stand must be adjusted by the performer himself; no one can put the hat of another on the head of the latter so as to be comfortable to him. The latter must pose it for himself. This law applies with peculiar force to music-stands.

The violinists proceed to tighten or slacken the hair of their bows, to throw back the coat collar, or stuff a white handkerchief under it, in order to adjust the violin to the peculiar crook of each neck, with as much apparent anxiety as if they had not been doing the same thing for the last thirty years, and some of their heads had not become bald over the sound-post. In the meantime, the other members of this well-bearded corps are streaming in with their instruments under the arm, and are placing their music books and lamps at the proper elevation on the stands, all the while talking, nodding, and smiling as if rehearsing half the day, and playing half the night, were a mighty good joke.

And then ascend to the highest parts of the house—to the regions of the operatic "paradise," those most singular of all instrumental sounds, those fifty or sixty antagonistic voluntaries with which all the audience would voluntarily dispense, consisting of chromatics in twenty different keys, violin octaves, harmonics, thirds and fifths, clarionet shakes, flute staccatos, horn growlings, ophicleide rumblings, triangular vibrations, and drum concussions.

> "See to their desks Apollo's sons repair—
> Swift rides the rosin o'er the horse's hair!
> In unison their various tones to tune,
> Murmurs the hautboy, growls the hoarse bassoon.
> In soft vibration sighs the whispering lute,
> Twang goes the harpsicord, too too the flute,
> Brays the loud trumpet, squeaks the fiddle sharp,
> Winds the French horn, and twangs the tingling harp."

About the time that the observer has made up in his mind an answer to the following mental queries—how many nights the first violinist could play without getting a crick in the neck—whether the flutist may not sometime blow his eyes so far out of his head that he may never be able to get them back again—how long it would take the operator on the *cornet à piston* to learn to play on the magnetic telegraph—why such a small man should be suffered to perform on such a big thing as an ophicleide, and how a person with such a huge moustache can get the piccola up to lips defended by such a bulwark of hair, a fermentation is observable in the midst of this musical whirlpool, which indicates the presence of some higher power. Place is given by the humble members of the orchestra, and the director is seen to stand forth in the attitude of mounting the tribunal from whence he guides his submissive subjects with despotic sway. He is a neat figured little man, with a profusion of methodically adjusted curls, a moustache that would render his physiognomy excessively ferocious, if an occasional smile playing over the distinguishable parts of his face, did not modify this expression. He is attired in the costume of the ball room, bearing in his button hole the most delicate rosebud of the conservatory, and in his perfectly gloved hand, an amber headed baton, the sceptre of command. At his appearance a wave of applause floats up from the audience, and the head and breast of the director bend down to meet it in a graceful and reverential bow, accompanied by a smile expressing the highest possible amount of inward gratification. This little acknowledgment of a becoming respect for the good opinion of the house is repeated once or twice, and then with the air of a man who has important business on hand, he mounts his elevated seat. He gives one or two magical taps on the stand, and the chaos of sounds is annihilated with the exception of the lamentations of one refractory violin, over which the owner has been for the last half hour repeatedly, first inclining his head in a horizontal position, and then tugging away at the screws. At this the director seems to be much annoyed, and the poor violinist, more annoyed, mutters to a companion that he wishes himself an *unspeakably* long way hence—probably in Italy where he could procure some good strings.

The resisting violin having been brought to subjection, the director casts an eye over the whole body of musicians, and having thrown back his head and lifted up both arms, very much in the supposed attitude of Ajax defying the thunder, he remains perfectly motionless for an instant, and then brings forward the whole of his body from the hips upwards, with a rapid and powerful jerk, which introduces his forehead into close proximity with the musical score which he pretends to be reading, the baton strikes the stand with a loud clap, and one old drummer proceeds to touch the drum, but in so gentle a manner, that it sounds as if, instead of using the sticks he were tossing some grains of shot on it. You now tremble for the safety of the director, and you enter into an arithmetical calculation with yourself, the basis of which is, that if the director by such a dangerous inclination of the person can only bring one poor drummer into movement, what amount of bodily labour he will be compelled to undergo, in order to operate on all that concourse of musicians. But your fears are dissipated in a few moments, for you discover that great sounds and little sounds are accompanied with about the same degree of gesticulatory emphasis. In the meantime some horns have commenced to blow on a very small scale, not hard enough, you would suppose, to drive the dust out of them, and if the piston of the cornet did not rattle so, you would pronounce its playing all a sham. The violins and flutes begin to be audible and the violinists are suddenly struck with a simultaneous desire to pick the strings, just as if that would make any music. All the other instruments are now doing duty in very feeble tones, and you take a look round the house to see who are there ; and you wonder why that particular family of Smiths, with whom you have the pleasure of an acquaintance has not yet appeared. You think Miss Julia Brown's hair arranged with the usual want of elegance, and then call to mind the fact that at Newport, the previous summer, you complimented her so many times on the peculiar taste which her coiffure always displayed. The aforesaid drummer is now giving the drum considerable ill usage, and then for the first time, you observe that he has two of them which he appears to beat alternately. The director is casting his head from one side to the other, flashes of disapprobation dart from his eyes upon the dilatory violinists, who from time to time, stop as it were, to catch breath, and fail to "come to the scratch" in due season. Every now and then a frown, dark as Erebus, spreads over his brow, as some poor laggard is astray in the mazes of sound, and can't find his place, or turns two pages instead of one, and consequently loses the thread of his harmonious discourse. The music grows so powerful that the conversation of the most enthusiastic and vociferous fast man no longer meets the ear. The orchestra is going as if they were riding an instrumental steeple chase, and the director looks more and more involved in doubt, as to which of his followers is to be left most in the rear.

At length when you have concluded that every musician has exhausted his last resource in the general attempt to make a noise, you are knocked into a start of astonishment by the introduction of a *corps de reserve,* in the clash of cymbals, which sounds as if a careless servant had stumbled in coming up stairs and smashed an entire set of Sevres china. In the midst of this carnage of crotchets and quavers, the director is obviously the controlling spirit who "rides in the whirlwind and directs the storm." There he sits producing no one sound except an occasional rap of his baton on the desk, and yet rousing to frenzy or lulling into tranquillity the instruments of all this tumult, every now and then, as Mr. Macaulay would say, "hurling foul scorn" at the heaps of little black dots that are crowded over the leaves of his score.

When the intensity of the tones has been diminished and augmented some half dozen times, the overture is concluded in four grand crashes, in which the cymbals make the most conspicuous figure. During the overture, however, there seems to be occasional seasons when there is a cessation of hostilities, and a soft plaintive air was taken up by one clarionet, violincello or oboe, with which air the audience must be very much delighted, for they laugh and talk with the greatest earnestness, and never turn their eyes towards the orchestra.

And now there is a new commotion among the musicians, while arranging every thing for the more serious undertaking, the opera itself. The director goes about like a general on the eve of battle, reconnoitres his forces, and marshals them for the attack. He mounts the elevated seat, gives another contortion to his frame, similar to that which was necessary to put the overture in movement, and then the curtain rises. Heads are slightly projected from the boxes at this movement, and many an alabaster neck is curved forward till the lowered drapery reveals the snowy bosom. The noise of conversation ceases, and the opera commences in earnest.

CHAPTER VIII.

Of the Opera in the Concrete.

"Lord! said my mother, what is all this story about?

"A cock and a bull, said Yorick—and one of the best of its kind I ever heard."—TRISTRAM SHANDY.

Prince Henry. "Wilt thou rob this leather-jerkin, crystal-button, nott-pated, agate-ring, puke stocking, caddis-garter, smooth-tongue, Spanish-pouch,—

Francis. "O Lord, sir, who do you mean?

P. Hen. "Why then, your brown bastard is your only drink: for, look you, Francis, your white canvass doublet will sully; in Barbary, sir, it cannot come to so much."—FIRST PART OF KING HENRY IV.

"If this were played upon a stage, now, I would condemn it as an improbable fiction."—TWELFTH NIGHT.

WHEN the curtain rises the scene represents a dark forest, where some quite well dressed, but desperate, foreign-looking gentlemen are engaged at a game of cards, which, from the abandoned appearance of the players, we are warranted to believe, must be some such low pastime as "all fours," or a hand at poker. The desperate gentlemen cantatorially inform the audience that their profession is that of outlaws, and remark that having no particular business then to engage them, they are staking quite extravagant sums on some cards, which the curious observer will discover to have a very unctuous appearance. How the outlaws ever came to be reduced to such straightened circumstances as to put up with these "lodgings upon the cold ground," or how they ever fell into such an improper course of life, we are not told, but we remember once hearing a fast man suggest that they were evidently "nobs who had overdrawn the badger by driving fast cattle, and going it high"—the exact signification of which words we did not understand, but supposed them to refer to scions of nobility who had squandered their patrimonies in riotous living. That these men are lost beyond the hope of redemption, is clear from the fact that they express their determination to employ themselves in no more useful or moral way; and how long they would persist in this pernicious amusement is rendered uncertain, by the entrance of their leader or chieftain—who, it is needless to say, is the tenor. From the first moment that the spectator casts his eye on this obviously unfortunate individual, he is at once interested in his case, observing to himself, that if the fellow is somewhat addicted to low company, still he's a very gentlemanly character, and to all appearance

> "The mildest manner'd man
> That ever scuttled ship or cut a throat."

His looks are sad and melancholy, and would indicate that he is either suffering from a cold in the head, or that his outlaws had been a little more successful at "all fours" than himself. The "dejected haviour of his visage" seems to touch the audience, for they immediately give him several rounds of applause, no doubt with the intention of raising his spirits. This kind manifestation of their feelings is responded to by one or two low bows, and then he turns towards his outlaws to obtain a becoming reception from them.

He is greeted by his followers with the greatest enthusiasm; though, to their inquiries after his health, he makes no reply, but walks languidly down to the foot-lights, and relates to both audience and outlaws, how deplorable will be his condition unless he receive the assistance of the latter in carrying out his designs. He goes on to state that the "voice of a certain damsel of Arragon has slid into his heart like dew upon a parched flower"—a simile which the reader will observe to be equally felicitous as novel. He adds, however, that a great old villain and tyrant (who of course must be the basso,) has carried off the Spanish maiden, and is about to compel her to marry him. The bandits become at once highly indignant, and with one accord seize their arms and declare that they will follow their chief to the castle of the old phylogynist, and *bouversé* all his designs by some insinuating digs of the poignard. The despondent chief seems comforted by this assurance of their "most distinguished consideration," and remarks that the young lady will no doubt be a consoling angel amidst the griefs of exile.

While he has been informing the audience and his friends of the state of his feelings, he has from time to time indulged in gestures about as strong as we can well conceive of, but now and then when an extraordinarily deep sentiment, and a very high note, choose the same moment for their expression, he is obliged to

poise himself on one foot, extend the other behind him, elevating the heel and depressing the toe, fold his hands over his breast, throw back the head and shake his body like a newfoundland dog just issuing from the water—the refractory note and the hidden emotion are always brought to light by these gesticulatory expedients.

Immediately after this, the scene having changed to the castle of the tyrant, the "Aragonese vergine" (the prima donna), is discovered reclining on an old box covered with green baize, which long-continued acquaintance with theatrical properties, enables the audience to recognize as a velvet *lounge.* This lady seems to be in great affliction, for which, however, we can discover no adequate cause, except that she is in such an unbecoming place for an unprotected female. The applause of the audience is overwhelming, and three very low, but extremely graceful and lady-like curtsies which she rises "to do," are the consequence.

The beaux are now in all the excitement that dandies dare permit themselves to yield to, alternately exclaiming, "how grand she is! how beautiful! heavens, but isn't she beautiful!" and then bringing down the focus of the opera-glass on the peerless woman.

The distressed female now launches off into a recitative, in which she expresses, in no measured terms, her utter aversion to the hateful old tyrant, and then falling on one knee, strikes into a cavatina, in which she says she hopes her lover, who necessarily must be the outlaw chief, (who again must necessarily be the tenor), will come immediately and run off with her—a wish that is probably often entertained by young ladies in reference to their particular lovers, but which is seldom avowed in this public way.

During the cavatina, she has been doing some very high singing, and making a great many of the newfoundland dog shakes, the lady part of the audience sitting wrapt in admiration, with the eyes fastened on the stage as intently as if they were witnessing a marriage ceremony, gently murmuring their approbation in detached sentences, such as "sweet, lovely, charming, exquisite;" while the fast men by the door, utter the words "knocker, fast nag," and declare that her time is "two thirty."

One of these very sporting young gentlemen asserts his readiness to "back her against the field." Just as the prima donna makes a very steep raise in the scale with a dreadful velocity of utterance, the same individual expresses his desire to withdraw the offer, observing that she is making her "brushes" too soon, and that he fears "she'll be too distressed to come home handsome."

A troupe of maidens with very plethoric ancles, now make their appearance, encumbered by large gilt paste-board caskets, containing some exceedingly brilliant paste-jewelry, intended as bridal presents for the unprotected female. They have, however, the strangest mode of offering these tokens of friendship that we have ever seen.

They arrange themselves in a line on one side of

the stage, apparently measuring their proximity to or distance from the foot-lights, with reference to the relative thickness of their ankles, until the lady nearest the audience seems to be the subject of a violent attack of elephantiasis. This done, they repeatedly sing five bars, and stretch out the right hand containing the present, in a line, forming, with the body, an angle of about ninety degrees.

A certain king of Castile in disguise, who is another of the many admirers of the heroine, breaks in on this little ceremony, expresses a strong wish to see her, and is told by one of the maidens, that the subject of his admirations is very much depressed in spirits, being considerably smitten with the afore-mentioned outlaw chieftain. The king is shocked at his adored one's want of taste in making a preference so little flattering to himself, and endeavours to force her to escape with him; but the young lady being highly indignant, draws a dagger, and threatens "to go into him," if he don't cease taking such liberties—thereby attracting considerable applause from some gentlemen in a back box, who have a strong penchant for dog-fighting. The outlaw happens to come in at the very nick of time, and after some quite serious altercation between him and the disguised king, at the moment when the "fancy" part of the audience are expecting a "set to," and admiring the courage of the little tenor (the outlaw), which they technically denominate the "game" of the "light weight," the heroine rushes between them with a drawn sword, threatening to destroy herself if they do not desist, and calling upon them to remember the honour of her mansion—thereby, no doubt, alluding to the possibility of an indictment for keeping a disorderly house.

The old tyrant, of whom we have heard a great deal, but have not as yet seen, returns home late at night to his castle, and finding two unknown gentlemen in his house without an invitation, conversing with his shut-up lady, he charges them with the impropriety of their behaviour. The strange gentlemen (the outlaw chief and the king in disguise), not particularly relishing these observations, beg him not to be so violent in his language. This seems only to incense the old fellow the more, who has just suggested "coffee and pistols," when the aforesaid king's followers entering, make the tyrant acquainted with the fact that he's been blowing up a king. The parasitical old tyrant immediately endeavours to excuse himself for the mistake he has made; says he hopes his royal highness will not be offended, that he had not the pleasure of his acquaintance, and all that sort of thing. The king rejoins that he is perfectly excuseable; that no offence has been done—that the cause of his own unlooked-for presence arises from the fact that he is out for the emperorship—that he is about doing a little electioneering, and that he just stopped in to learn the state of public feeling in his district, and solicit his (the tyrant's) vote. The tyrant being a good deal flattered by this appeal to his chief weak point—namely, his own fancied knowledge of party politics—says that the king does him great honour—"supreme honour"—and invites him to spend the night in the castle; which kind invitation his majesty graciously accepts.

In the meantime, the outlaw, having observed how much more cordially the tyrant is received than himself, has made his exit. The king's followers all draw up in line and conclude the act by a song, the burden of which is that their master's nomination is the only one "fit to be made."

The next act discovers the tyrant awaiting the arrival of the unfortunate heroine, to whom he is going to be married in a few minutes. All is jollity in the castle, till a gentleman clothed as a pilgrim, interrupts the general hilarity; for when the bride enters, he throws off the dreadful black cloak and reveals the outlaw chieftain. He pitches himself into a variety of passionate attitudes, to the great terror of a whole boarding school of young ladies, whom their teacher has permitted to visit the opera to improve their style of singing. The bride elect rushes up to him, and so they both step down to the foot-lights. The outlaw gentleman passes his right hand round the waist of the lady, and clasps in his left both of her's, elevating them to a line with the breast. They remain stationary for a moment, whilst the orchestra is playing the symphony, looking as fondly into each other's eyes as a pair of dear little turtle doves, and smiling as sweetly as every gentleman and lady have a right to smile under such pleasant circumstances. There they begin to assure each other simultaneously of the pleasure they would find in immediately dying, placed in the attitude which they are at present enjoying so highly; by a rare and curious accident, both repeating the same words, with the exception of the respective substitution of the pronouns "I, you, my, your, he, she," as often as such substitutions become necessary—as if one should say, for example,

I'll You'll	bet	my your	money on the bob-tail mare.
He'll She'll	bet	his her	money on the bob-tail mare.

The outlaw is, however, obliged to run and hide himself, because he hears the king knocking to come in, and he fears that he'll be killed if he is discovered. The king enters, and with a very "fee, fi, fo, fum" air, asks for the body of the outlaw. The tyrant tells a most bare-faced falsehood, swears the outlaw is not in his house, and so, the king, after considerable use of the word wretch, traitor, menditore, &c., carries off the bride as a hostage, to the great chagrin of the tyrant. As soon as the king has departed with his fair companion, the tyrant runs to the outlaw's hiding place, and dragging him forth by the collar, declares that he'll kill him himself. The outlaw, under great excitement, seizes his head in both hands in a manner so terrible, that self-decapitation would seem to be inevitable, which so alarms the aforesaid boarding school misses, that two of them go off into hysterics, and they are carried into the lobby, where the cutting of their laces is attended with an explosion similar to that of "popping" a champagne cork. The outlaw prays the tyrant not to kill him just now, and says he will give him permission to do so at any future period. "Here, sir," adds he, still addressing himself to the tyrant, "is a very fine *cornet á piston*, allow me to present it to you with the assurance, that whenever you wish to obtain my presence for the purpose of exterminating me, you will merely be obliged to sound the note of B flat, and I will unhesitatingly cómply with your wishes." In the words of the poet Tennyson,

> "Leave me here, and when you want me,
> Sound upon the bugle horn."

The tyrant accepts the present upon the accompanying condition, but having no great confidence in the word of a man who has been associating so long a time with bad company, he requires him to make oath to that effect; which being done, both gentlemen call upon the chorus to follow them immediately in pursuit of the king and his captive lady. These cowardly rascals stand some five minutes and sing about their readiness to depart, instead of marching off instantly, as they are requested to do.

In the third act, the king hides himself in a grave-yard during the election for emperor, probably out of fear that he may be defeated. While wandering among the grave-stones he overhears some of his political enemies, (among whom is the outlaw chieftain,) plotting his assassination. The conspirators cast lots for the office of assassin, and the lot *very naturally* falls on the outlaw. The next moment the report of cannon is heard, and the king's retinue come in, bringing with them the heroine—who, we must confess, seems to have no real business there,—and state that the polls have closed, and that the king has been elected emperor. Thereupon the new emperor calls the conspirators up and is about to have them killed, just as it might be expected an emperor would do.

The heroine begs for the life of the miserable

offenders, telling the emperor that if he wishes to be considered a sovereign of respectability, and not conduct himself like one who had "stolen a precious diadem and put it in his pocket," he must pardon the delinquents. The emperor relents, and pronounces a pardon for the conspirators. He calls up the robber chieftain and the heroine, and uniting their hands, expresses an ardent wish that they may, as the libretto says, "love forever." The pleasure of the two lovers is indescribable, and the whole company begin to sing the praises of such a trump of an emperor. The air, which is chosen as the vehicle to carry all this adulation to royal ears, is apparently one of those crashing, clashing passages in the overture; and if the emperor does not hear the voice of flattery, it is because the gentlemen who preside over the kettle-drum and cymbals, seem to have entered into a conspiracy to prevent it. The more zealous the chorus is in its efforts to make an agreeable impression on their sovereign, and the louder the voice is raised for this object, the more that irritable old drummer seems anxious to defeat their sycophantic purposes. If you are one of those excitable persons who are prone to take a side in every contest that comes under their observation, whether it be two gentlemen running for the presidency, or two bull-terriers "punishing" each other for the possession of a bone, you immediately determine who you hope may carry their point. In your admiration of the dogged perseverance of the old drummer, you take part in favour of the instruments, and when you hear that sudden and awful clash of the cymbals, which causes you to start till you dig your elbow into an elderly gentleman on one side, and tread on some corny toes on the other, you felicitate yourself upon the victory of parchment and brass over throats; but the next moment your pleasure is extinguished, for the tenor and soprano give their voices an extra lift, and away they go up like rockets, far aloft above the din of horns, cymbals and kettle drums.

The fourth and last act represents the terrace of a highly illuminated palace, which may be seen in the back ground. Some masked gentlemen, very bandy-legged and knock-kneed, dressed in tight hose, well calculated to exhibit these deformities, are observed flirting with some of the before mentioned thick-ankled ladies, who likewise rejoice in dominos. Every thing indicates that this is a place, where people are in the habit of being extremely jolly, and from which such stupid things as parties to which a few friends are invited "very sociably", or family re-unions, are entirely abolished. Presently all the company break out with the expression of one general wish for the unbounded prosperity of the outlaw chief and the heroine whom we saw betrothed in the last act, and who have just been married. They make their exit shortly afterward in great precipitation, having been frightened from the stage by the appearance of a great, horrible-looking figure, clothed in black, which seems to be a species of bug-bear, sent to scare such naughty people who do nothing but dance, sing and make merry. The bug-bear exits shortly after.

Again the highly profligate chorus enter, in no wise corrected by the visitation of the gloomy looking gentleman, and assure the audience what a pleasant thing it is for one man to flirt with another's wife from behind a mask, or for an innocent young lady "going her first winter" to whisper in a corner with a man about town ; but getting weary of this occupation, they at last retire, and the newly married couple—the outlaw and his bride—again show themselves.

The outlaw seems to be struck with a highly poetic vein, for he tells the lady that the noise of the polka in the palace has ceased, that the gas has been stopped off, and that the stars are amusing themselves by smiling on their happy union, "because they've nothing else to do." Thereupon they indulge in a gentle embrace, and start off simultaneously in a duo, declaratory of the union of their two hearts in such an anti-anatomical manner, that henceforth until their latest breath, one cardiacal organ will suffice to perform the functions of two separate bodies. Scarcely have they made this declaration of their abnormal heart-union, before the sound of a horn falls on the ears of the o'er happy couple. At this moment the outlaw forgets all good breeding, and still influenced by his former brigand habits, swears a most horrible oath in the presence of his young bride, and seems to be overcome by great depression of spirits. The poor woman, observing nothing singular about the blast of the horn—in all probability fancying that it is only the tooting of a lazy post boy somewhat behind time, prays him to cheer up, and let her see him smile. Before the outlaw can comply with this small request the horn sounds again. "Behold," shrieks the young husband, "the tiger seeks his prey." The bride surveys the apartment, but observing no tiger or other ferocious animal, takes it for granted that he has the mania à potu, induced by imbibing too much champagne at the wedding feast. She immediately runs out into the bridal chamber, with the intention of putting on those indefinite garments denominated "things," and going to call up the court physician. The outlaw chieftain stands a moment listening with breathless attention, and hearing no more of the horn, comes to the conclusion that he has no just ground for fear, and that it was only a dreadful ringing in the ears with which he is sometimes afflicted. He thereupon rushes in pursuit of his bride, but just as he arrives at the door of the bridal chamber, his progress is arrested by the same black hob-goblin gentlemen who frighted the dissipated chorus, as before related. This gentleman is recognized by the outlaw in spite of his black clothes and mask, as the hateful old tyrant who persecuted him to such an extent some time previously. The outlaw groans a few times, and then the tyrant asks his victim if he calls to mind his promise, and the words of the poet Tennyson,

> "Leave me here, and when you want me
> Sound upon the bugle horn."

The poor outlaw begs for his life; but the old tyrant remains inexorable, and tells him that he must die.

The unhappy bride returns, and hearing her husband entreating the old tyrant so fervently for a respite, unites her supplications with those of her husband. To this the tyrant makes no direct answer, but merely presents a poignard to the trembling outlaw, with a repetition of the words of the poet Tennyson.

> "Leave me here, and when you want me
> Sound upon the bugle horn."

The outlaw perceiving no mode of escaping from this *horn* of the dilemma, seizes the poignard, drives it in his breast, and sinks mortally wounded. The poor bride shrieks, and falls upon his body. Now succeeds a scene of pulling and dragging on the floor. The wounded tenor is called upon to struggle and writhe in all the agonies of death, and the prima donna to follow him up in order to raise his head on her knee, and thus give him an opportunity of singing his dying solo. To do this in such a manner as not to render the whole thing ridiculous and farcical, instead of tragic and touching, requires all the grace and ease imaginable. When well done it is impressive; when badly it is laughable; but whether touching or laughable, it is sure to be relished by a large part of the audience, for it always discloses who has done most for the prima donna's bust, dame nature or the mantua maker.

The tenor's head being elevated to the proper height, he expresses it as his dying wish that the prima donna will continue to live and cherish his memory. They then lament their unhappy fate in a short duo. The tenor dies; the prima donna appears to do the same, but the libretto consoles you by declaring that she only swoons. The old tyrant—the basso—chuckles like a wretch over the success of his successful plot, declares it a revenge worthy of a demon; you concur in his sentiments, and the curtain falls.

Gentle reader, are you wearied out with this insufferable nonsense? Do not say that you are, or you will have established a reputation for want of taste, beyond all controversy. Not to admire what we have written in this chapter, is to condemn what we know you have often declared was a "love of an opera." We have merely explained the plot of a well known operatic *chef d' œuvre*, which, goodness knows, required an explanation.

Now do not be petulant, and *very satirically* exclaim,—"I wish he would explain his explanation," thereby showing, both that you can be excessively severe, and that you have read Byron. We do not intend to endeavour to render luminous that which is so very clear and evident in its meaning; it would be to "gild refined gold," and all that sort of thing, and therefore we spare you the infliction.

CHAPTER IX.

Après.

I'm fond of fire and crickets, and all that,
A lobster salad, and champagne, and chat.
BYRON.

From this genteel place the reader must not be surprised, if I should convey him to a cellar, or a common porter-house.
CONNOISSEUR. No. 1.

Sweet is old wine in bottles, ale in barrels.
BYRON.

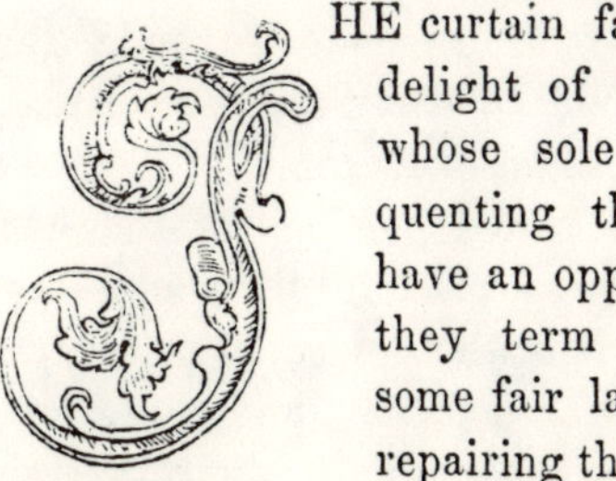

HE curtain falls, much to the delight of those gentlemen whose sole motive for frequenting the opera, is to have an opportunity of what they term "chaffing" with some fair lady friend, whilst repairing thither, and returning from thence, as well as duriug the enchanting moments when the "drop" displays one of those accommodating landscapes, which the audience, at their option, may convert either into the lake of Como, or the ruins of Palmyra. If we may trust the assertion of many fair mouths, we must infer that the curtain has fallen, much to the regret of certain young ladies who declare that they could sit and hear Bosio forever—a period of time which we have always been taught to regard as very long indeed.

But the curtain *has* fallen, and the gentlemen who have been foolish enough to send *bouquets* to the prima donna in the morning, all seem suddenly to be struck with the bright idea, that by giving a few knocks of a cane, or a few taps of a gloved hand, they can "call out" that divine woman, and by some adroit manœuvre render themselves distinguishable, and obvious to her from out that mass of heads and black coats. The persons who occupy the elevated portions of the house, who have paid a small price for their admittance, like all other persons who pay small prices, make large demands for their money, and consequently unite with the prima donna's admirers in an attempt to get a last, long, lingering look at the lady. They really "do" all the applause, thundering with their heavy canes and beating their hands together until they resemble small lumps of crude beef steaks. After the requisite amount of delay which is imposed upon the audience to give them an adequate idea of the obligation the prima donna will confer, should she see fit to exhibit herself, a human head is seen to project from behind the curtain, but is drawn back with that kind of jerk which is said to be peculiar to a turtle establishing his right to the homestead exemption. This little *aiguillon* of the prompter has the desired effect, for the gentlemen in the parquette, who expect the prima donna to observe *them* to the entire exclusion of the other five hundred men in white cravats and black coats, become perfectly frantic, and the sojourners in "paradise" threaten to take advantage of their position and empty themselves on the heads of the higher orders of society, who happen for the present to be below them. The excitement now begins to infuse itself into all present; the most apathetic old *habitués* commence to stretch forth their necks, to wriggle on their seats, and manifest other signs of sympathy, with the more inflammable portion of the audience. At length the tenor comes forward from the side of the curtain, with a sickly smile of inexpressible pleasure on his countenance. He leads by the hand the prima donna, whose downcast eyes, and modest demeanor, entirely mislead the audience, giving them the fullest assurance of her "beauiful disposition," and wholly contradicting the assertion that she ever stamps her foot at the leader, or tears the hair of her maid. The brace of singers make one acknowledgment of gratitude immediately after issuing from behind the ruins of Palmyra, thence proceeding in front of said ruins, make another, and the moment before their disappearance perpetrate a third. This is not sufficient for those enamoured ones who think that by some evident mistake the prima donna has not recognised *them*, so the patting of gloves and the tapping of canes is again resorted to, which, together with the efforts of the "upper circles," again extracts the tenor and his "inamorata" together with the drowsy basso. The last-named person wears an air of great reluctance at thus being detained on the stage, instead of being permitted to go home to his *patés* and *fricasées*. The three go through the reverential with due regard to time and position, and then withdraw, leaving the house to contemplate the gas light, and reflect upon the briefness of all human pleasures.

During all this time the ladies have been standing in an apparently half decided state, as to what was ultimately to become of them, alternately looking on the stage and picking up hoods and shawls which they immediately let fall again. Now that their suspense is ended, they commence to hood and shawl; and many is the gentleman who announces in whispers that he is unspeakably happy in being permitted to place a cloak upon shoulders that rival alabaster.

Harry Brown is unfortunate, for Miss Smith's cousin George has anticipated him, having already astutely seized upon a shawl, during the "calling out" which he carefully keeps until the blissful moment arrives for enveloping that lady. Miss Smith thanks cousin George, as she always calls him, with such a sweet smile that Harry Brown immediately becomes occupied in a protracted search after his hat, muttering to himself "hang these cousins."

The audience go out of the boxes together with

the going out of the gas, and masses of people stand crowded together in the lobbies, while the house is slowly emptying itself.

The fast-men have collected about in front of the different box doors from which the ladies are issuing, and are examining the relative claims to beauty, which the fair observed ones merit, or as they term it, "are getting their points." They are heard to make their comparisons upon the singers too, with all the assurance of the old *habitués*, telling about Salvi's falsetto, and Bettini's chest-voice, with a wondrous deal of volubility. Where the crowds from the upper tiers unite with those of the lower, one loud-voiced critic, who has just made his descent, is heard to observe to a friend that "though Salvi is an old cock, he is nevertheless a remarkably sound egg;" but why such a peculiarly gallinaceous reference is made to that distinguished tenor, we must unhesitatingly confess ignorance.

After the confusion attendant on the coming and going of carriages, cabs and divers other vehicles, the fatigued audience are at length set in motion towards their respective dwellings.

Again poor Harry Brown is a fit subject for

our commiseration. The ill-fated young man is placed by the side of Miss Smith's mother, a rather antique lady; Cousin George somehow or other, has managed to place himself beside Miss Smith. The carriage passes a lamp-post, and though Harry Brown does observe Cousin George's left hand, the disappearance of the right is something for which he cannot at all account, except upon the laws of proximity which pertain to cousinship. While the carriage proceeds homewards the party does not converse as freely as they did a short time before, under the exhilaration arising from gas-light and gossip. Harry Brown finds the ride a bore, Mrs. Smith is so deaf, and still has her ideas of public amusement, confined to the times when Mr. Kemble, Mr. Cooper and Mr. Cooke, performed in the *legitimate drama* to crowded bouses. Cousin George's position is such a happy one, that conversation is to him a thing superfluous.

Those whose means authorise them, and very often those whose means do not authorise them, go home to a nice supper, some delicate partridges, cold capon, or deviled turkey, and a bottle or two of champagne. Under the influences of the warm room and the viands, not to mention that "warm champagny, old particular brandy-punchy feeling" induced by the popping cork, the events of the whole evening are reviewed in a quite thorough manner, though without much attention to a "*lucidus ordo.*"

Let us follow the Smiths home, and see what is their mode of terminating the evening. Scarcely have they settled themselves at table before a glass of champagne is administered all round, and a very severe criticism of Bosio is commenced by Cousin George, who says in a very opinionated way, that he likes her pretty well, but prefers either Truffi or Stefanoni. Miss Smith immediately espouses the cause of the injured Bosio, whom she has often declared she could listen to "forever," and calls on Harry Brown to come to the rescue of the cantatrice's reputation. Harry, who has been sadly silent ever since the miraculous disappearance of Cousin George's right hand in the carriage, at once becomes a violent Bosioite, and maintains the vocal abilities of that prima donna against the whole world; whereupon Miss Smith with one of the most approving of smiles, exclaims, "Thank you, Mr. Brown; I always knew you were a gentleman of taste. There, there, let me shake hands with you." And as Miss Smith utters the last words, she extends such a ridiculously little hand across the table, that it seems almost a misnomer to apply that appellation to it. Mr. Brown seizes the proffered member, and gives it as hearty a pressure as the publicity of the occasion will permit. From the moment that he touches the magical little hand, cousin George is eclipsed. Harry's knowledge of operas, music and singers, becomes at once astonishingly enlarged, and he speaks on operatic subjects like one having authority to do so. Fortunately for cousin George, Miss Smith's brother Charles enters, his clothes strongly redolent of Havannahs, he having just returned from his club. His sister forbids him to come so near her, alleging as a ground for such a prohibition, that those "horrid" cigars are *so* offensive to her. Her brother moves good naturedly to the other side of the table, having first applied his finger to his sister's cheek in a playful way, which has a powerful effect upon poor Harry, causing him to feel exceedingly as if he should like to do the same thing himself. The sister begins to assure her brother of the inestimable amount of pleasure he has lost by loitering at the "horrid" club, instead of accompanying her to the *delicious* opera. The reply is that "the club" has voted Bosio a bore, and that consequently he cannot think of wasting his valuable time by going to hear her. The sister then makes some very severe remarks upon clubs in the abstract, but is interrupted by her brother's inquiring if she does not want to take a share in the great stakes which the club is endeavouring to raise, in order to *pit* Tom Hyer against Harry Broome the English champion. The sister pretends to be so provoked at the *raillerie* of her brother, that she smiles in a way that makes her look doubly pretty, calls him a "horrid creature," then turns to Harry Brown and indulges in some rather pointed observations, relative to divers of the good people who were among the audience at the opera.

Mrs. Smith, who has up to this moment been very laudably occupied in seeing that the young people get a due proportion of the well selected viands, now comes in for a part of the conversation. She, good lady, knows the fathers and grandfathers, mothers and grandmothers, of the present generation, and can tell just what amount of homage each of the dashing families of the city have a right to lay claim to. She declares that Mrs. Simms has no right to assume the importance that she does—that though her father was a very respectable man, still, when she was a girl, the family lived in a very obscure part of the town, and were wholly unknown among our first people. Miss Smith, however, who is very much afraid that her mother is going to indulge in too minute and wearisome an investigation of genealogies, conducts the conversation to subjects which she supposes to be more interesting to the rest of the party. She objects to the want of taste displayed by those awful looking Misses Rogers, who deck themselves out like young girls, when every body knows they have been in society for the last fifteen years—that their mother has made herself notorious, as well as ridiculous, by angling for every young man of desirable means in the city. Miss Smith likewise expresses her wonder when that stupid Lieutenant Jones *will* marry Miss Simms. She declares that "she is tired of seeing the two together; that one cannot go to any public place, but the first persons who meet the eye are Jones and Miss Simms; that if the weather is fair, and you walk out, there are the loving couple in the street. Go to Newport, there they are—go to the opera, there they are. If they can find means to run incessantly to parties and balls, watering places and operas, why cannot they get married?" Miss Smith concludes her observations on the over-fond lovers, by emphasising the words "so stupid, is it not?" at the same time giving them both an affirmative and interrogative character. Harry Brown responds that it might be excessively uninteresting to be always thus placed in proximity to Miss Simms, but that there are other young ladies of his acquaintance, with whom such extreme intimacy would be any thing but stupid. To this ambiguous use of the word "stupid," Miss Smith makes no reply, but merely looks at Mr. Brown as if she had not the slightest idea whatever that a very personal allusion to herself, had been made by that gentleman. Miss Smith again indulges in reflections on society with a great deal of freedom and pointedness of expression, which much amuses cousin George, who laughs approvingly at what he terms the "sharpness" of his relative. Brother Charles remains wholly unattentive to a kind of conversation which his fair sister so often takes part in, and is absorbed in estimating, on the back of a visiting card, the probability of his winning his bet on the late election. Harry Brown, after his complimentary effort, sinks into a state of silence, induced by the loquacity of Miss Smith, the hilarity of cousin George, and the negligence of brother Charles. Alas for Harry! he is considering the likelihood that such a censorious young lady can have a kind heart—or would make a good wife. At this moment, Mr. Smith, Senior, walks into the dining-room. A worthy, respectable, and well-to-do man is Mr. Smith, the elder; he pays his taxes and he loves his children, and who can do more? Miss Smith immediately rises from the table, puts up her dear little mouth to her papa to be kissed. The tender parent goes through the osculatory process in such an affectionate manner, that Harry Brown is strongly impressed with the idea that the old gentleman would make a trump of a father-in-law, and he begins to suspect that Miss Smith's heart is not so bad after all. The elderly Smith takes his seat, having first shaken Harry by the hand in a friendly, familiar way, that indicates a very good opinion of that worthy young person. The conversation again reverts to operatics, but Harry seems to have forgotten all his late familiarity with such subjects, and becomes suddenly very conversant with rail-roads, canals and stocks, and launches out into an earnest conversation with Mr. Smith on those interesting topics.

But everything must have an end, and so about midnight Mr. Brown *walks* home through a foot of snow, because his mind is too much occupied with thoughts of Miss Smith and her cousin George, to allow him to think of calling a cab.

Let us now see what becomes of those gentlemen who have been sitting in the parquette, giving the opera their most anxious attention at all such times as either the prima donna is on the stage, or any aria is sung, but who have been giving quite unmistakeable signs of ennui and weariness during the recitatives and choruses. If we have narrowly observed the movements of this portion of the audience, we will have remarked, that during the performance of the last act they have, from time to time, cast hurried glances towards the avenues of egress, and contorted their countenances in a way which would indicate that their olfactories were greeted by certain savory odours, imperceptible to every body but the possessors of the said olfactories. These gentlemen, immediately after leaving the opera, may be seen to walk along the street in companies of three or four, with a hurried step, until their progress is arrested by the view of divers green, blue, pink, or crimson coloured lamps, holding a very conspicuous position over the doors of some houses of very suggestive exterior, or before some suspicious hiatuses in the pavement, where those horrid monsters, who figure in Christmas pantomimes, might easily be imagined to dwell. These lamps seem to be possessed of a most incredible power of human attraction, for no sooner does their light fall upon the vision of the nocturnal wayfarer, than he is drawn within the portals over which they are established. Upon mounting the steps into these houses, or descending into these subterranean regions, the inquirer will discover a long, brilliantly illuminated, gaudily papered chamber, whose walls are ornamented with numerous over-grown mirrors, and French coloured prints, representing young ladies in short dresses, standing in every possible posture except that usually assumed by ladies of our acquaintance. Along one side of this apartment, at the distance of about three and a half feet from the wall, extends a marble slab, placed in a horizontal position, and elevated three feet from the floor, forming a species of enclosure. Within this enclosure, a number of men, habited to the waist in white garments,—apparently a nameless order of priesthood—are going through some inexplicable mystic rites, repeatedly seizing up various large glass bottles containing transparent or opaque liquids, and carrying them to different parts of this marble slab at the request of various persons, who seem to be the worshippers in this temple. At one end of the enclosure, a solitary man of a dark and sombre hue, evidently a person held more sacred than the other priests, is seen alternately to hammer portions of some hard matter, resembling stone in appearance, and then split them by the magical application of a small piece of blunt iron. He conducts this ceremony with the greatest solemnity, occasionally pronouncing these incantatory words, "Plate or shell, sah?" in a seemingly interrogative manner. The worshippers at these shrines are some of the same young gentlemen whom we have seen standing back in the opera boxes by the doors, making fast remarks on all that was passing around them, or sitting in the parquette endeavouring to annihilate the prima donna by the attractiveness of their appearance. Others, of this same class of persons, merely pass through this chamber, having first said in a low tone to the most potential of the priests, "Four dozen broiled; ale for one, and brandy and water for three." The priest immediately repeats these words so fraught with significance, in a loud voice, which resounds through the whole chamber. An invisible priest, at some distance from the first, again repeats them, and thus the mysterious sound is passed from one unseen priest to another, until it ceases to be heard in the distance.

Nothing more is seen of the last described devotees, for some time after their leaving the mysterious apartment; but about midnight a confused sound of human voices is heard to issue from another mysterious chamber. Some of those voices express a dogged determination on the part of their proprietors, to remain shut up within the present confines until the matutinal hours; other voices assure a universal confidence in the powers of a certain bob-tail mare, while one teaches in the Italian language the secret of ever living happily.* At between two and three o'clock in the morning, several of our *operators* are seen to emerge from the aforesaid houses and subterranean abodes, in a very musical, as well as affectionate frame of mind. One gentleman, totally regardless of the lateness of the hour, after manifesting a strong desire to embrace a large party of his friends, kindly invites them home to take tea with him. Another walks homeward, expressing his notions on the secret of living happily in a cantatory way. A third is assisted into a cab by his associates, with directions to the driver to set him down at his lodgings. Arrived there, he is put to bed, when he dreams that he is falling down five hundred precipices; that afterwards a huge man is on the point of cutting off his head, but a very

* Il segreto per esser felici.

prima donna like looking lady comes in and intercedes for him, and she thus saves his life; that he is just going to be married to the prima donna like looking lady, when his pleasure is interrupted by the sound of ten thousand horns, each one four times as large as that he saw the tyrant have in the opera; whereupon he awakes, and discovers that there is a cry of fire, and the firemen are making almost as much noise as the orchestra did, when it was doing the crashing passages.

* * * * *

In the morning, the chambermaid wonders why Mr. Higgins rings for water, when she recollects filling the ewer full the night previous. Next day Mr. Higgins examines his operatic accounts, and finds them to stand thus:

To one pair kid gloves, .	$1.00
" opera ticket, (secured seat,)	1.50
" supper, . . .	3.00
" cab-hire, ...	1.00
Total,	6.50

At that moment his land-lady sends in the bill

for lodging, which, by-the-by, she always seems to do when he is in one of his repentant moods, and Mr. Higgins expresses a kind wish that all Italians were in a climate somewhat warmer than that of the south of Europe.

The Smiths do not feel any inconvenience, physical or pecuniary, from their visit to the opera, and *petit souper* afterwards. "When one has money," says Mrs. Smith, in a very oracular tone, "what is the use of it, except to let people know that one has got it!" Immediately after this expression of her sentiments in regard to filthy lucre, Mrs. Smith tells the servant not to give a shilling to the whimpering little boy who has been sweeping the snow off the pavement; that a sixpence is enough, and more than enough, for him, and that it is wrong to encourage such exorbitance.

* * * * *

Now, that Mr. Higgins should feel thirsty in the morning, or that Mrs. Smith should regret to part with a sixpence, concerns not us; we have not been writing to correct public morals, but only to amuse the readers of THE PHYSIOLOGY OF THE OPERA.

ERRATA.

Page.	Line.	
16	6	after a, insert *fast man or a.*
34	10	" chef (d' orchestre), read *chef d' orchestre.*
34	17	" chef (d' orchestre), " *chef d' orchestre.*
55	10	" guoi, read *quoi.*
55	10	" singers, read *Singers.*
55	11	" led horse, read *lead horse.*
70	24	" was, read *is.*
76	12	" bulversé, read *boulversé.*
92	22	" gentlemen, read *gentleman.*

D. W. Krummel is Professor of Library Science and of Music at the University of Illinois in Urbana, where his specialties include research library collection development and historical bibliography, as well as American music bibliography and music printing. A 1976 Guggenheim Fellow, he was formerly Associate Librarian of the Newberry Library in Chicago and is President of the Music Library Association, 1981-83. His research activities have included a series of articles in the *Yearbook for Inter-American Musical Research*, 1971-75, as well as the general supervision of the project which produced *Resources of American Music History* (Urbana: University of Illinois Press, 1981).